Grasslands

Lily Erlic

WEIGL PUBLISHERS INC.

Published by Weigl Publishers Inc.
350 5th Avenue, Suite 3304, PMB 6G
New York, NY 10118-0069

Web site: www.weigl.com

Library of Congress Cataloging-in-Publication Data

Erlic, Lily.
Grasslands / Lily Erlic.
p. cm. — (Biomes)
Includes index.
ISBN 978-1-59036-346-1 (hard cover : alk. paper) ISBN 978-1-59036-352-2 (soft cover : alk. paper)
1. Grassland ecology—Juvenile literature. I. Title. II. Biomes (Weigl Publishers)
QH541.5.P7E75 2006 577.4—dc22 2005004391

Printed in the United States of America
3 4 5 6 7 8 9 0 12 11 10 09 08

Photograph Credits
Every reasonable effort has been made to trace ownership and to obtain permission to reprint copyright material. The publishers would be pleased to have any errors or omissions brought to their attention so that they may be corrected in subsequent printings.

Cover: Getty Images/Brand X Pictures (front); Getty Images/Nicholas Parfitt/Stone (back left); Getty Images/Lester Lefkowitz/Photographer's Choice (back middle); Getty Images/Belinda Wright/National Geographic (back right).

Getty Images: pages 1 (Farrell Grehan/National Geographic), 3 (Lester Lefkowitz/Photographer's Choice), 4 (Robert Glusic/Photodisc Green), 5 (Darrell Gulin/The Image Bank), 6 (Tom Bean/The Image Bank), 7L (Brand X Pictures), 7R (George Grall/National Geographic), 10 (Oliver Strewe/Stone), 11T (Annie Griffiths Belt/National Geographic), 11B (Neil Emmerson/Robert Harding World Imagery), 12 (Terry Donnelly/The Image Bank), 13L (Photodisc Blue), 13R (Beverly Joubert/National Geographic), 14 (Ed Young/FoodPix), 15L (Chris Salvo/Taxi), 15R (Phil Degginger/Stone), 16L (Frank Oberle/Stone), 16R (Brand X Pictures), 17T (Darrell Gulin/Photographer's Choice), 17B (altrendo nature/Altrendo), 18L (Mattias Klum/National Geographic), 18R (Taesam Do/Botanica), 19R (James Randklev/The Image Bank), 19L (Thomas Schmitt/The Image Bank), 20L (Mimotito/Digital Vision), 20R (Photodisc Blue), 21L (Joel Sartore/National Geographic), 21R (Nicole Duplaix/National Geographic), 22L (Nicholas Parfitt/Stone), 22R (Photodisc Blue), 23L (Stan Osolinski/Taxi), 23R (John Giustina/Taxi), 24 (Belinda Wright/National Geographic), 25 (Frank Herholdt/Stone), 26 (Digital Vision), 27L (John Lamb/Stone), 27R (Beth Wald/Aurora), 28 (Oliver Strewe/Stone), 29T (Frank Greenway/Dorling Kindersley), 29B (Photodisc Blue), 30 (Julie Toy/The Image Bank).

Project Coordinators Heather C. Hudak, Heather Kissock

Substantive Editor Tina Schwartzenberger

Copy Editor Heather Kissock

Designers Warren Clark, Janine Vangool

Photo Researchers Heather C. Hudak, Kim Winiski

Cover description: Grasslands are dominated by large areas of grass, and contain few trees and large shrubs. The area of grasslands expands as hotter and drier temperatures dominate.

CONTENTS

Introduction

Earth is home to millions of different **organisms,** all of which have specific survival needs. These organisms rely on their environment, or the place where they live, for their survival. All plants and animals have relationships with their environment. They interact with the environment itself, as well as other plants and animals within the environment. This interaction creates an **ecosystem.**

Different organisms have different needs. Not every animal can survive in extreme climates. Not all plants require the same amount of water. Earth is composed of many types of environments, each of which provides organisms with the living conditions they need to survive. Organisms with similar environmental needs form communities in areas that meet these needs. These areas are called biomes. A biome can have several ecosystems.

One-quarter of Earth's surface is covered in grasslands. The grasslands biome can be found in the center of large continents or alongside large deserts. Grasslands located near the equator have very hot climates, so the grass is dry.

There are two main types of grasslands—savanna and temperate. Savannas, or tropical grasslands, consist mainly of grass and a few trees and shrubs. Savanna is located in parts of Australia, central South America, central and South Africa, and some parts of India. In central Africa, savanna covers 5 million square miles (13 million square kilometers).

Grasslands can be identified as large, open areas covered with grass and small plants.

Temperate grasslands are similar to tropical grasslands, but with fewer trees. Temperate grasslands cover large areas on many continents. One of the largest temperate grasslands is the Eurasia steppe in Russia. Prairie grassland covers the land near the Rocky and Appalachian Mountains in North America. Temperate grasslands can also be found in southern Australia and in parts of South America.

FASCINATING FACTS

In South America, there are many large savannas. Llanos, in the Orinoco River basin, is as large as the state of Texas.

Earth has 14 million square miles (36 million sq km) of grasslands.

Grevy's zebras are often found in savannas and the plains.

World Grasslands

Every continent in the world contains grasslands except Antarctica. Grasslands are located in five main areas. These are the prairies of North America, the steppes of central Eurasia, the veldt of South Africa, the deserts in Australia, and the pampas of South America.

In North America, three types of prairie dominate the United States and Canada. Tall-grass prairie is located in the eastern part of the midwestern United States. Its grass grows up to 5 feet (1.5 meters) tall. The short grass is located in the western part of the midwest United States and in Canada. Short grass grows less than 2 feet (61 centimeters) high. Mixed grass grows to be 2 to 3 feet (61 to 91 cm) tall. This type of grassland is found in the center of the midwestern United States.

Sheyenne National grassland in North Dakota extends over 70,000 acres (28,000 hectares), providing habitats to some uncommon animal species and plants.

Eurasia's grasslands spread from western Russia over to central Asia. In southern Africa, the veldt grasslands grow on higher ground. Much of South America's pampas are located in eastern Argentina. Australia's temperate grasslands, or rangelands, are found mainly in the southeast part of the continent. The tropical grasslands of Australia are found in the north.

Fountain grass, often regarded as a weed, can grow up to 3 feet (0.91 m) tall, and is often found in deserts and grasslands.

FASCINATING FACTS

The roots of tall grass can extend 9 feet (2.7 m) below ground. When the roots die, they become organic matter that feeds the soil.

Prairie grasses come in many colors, including red, purple, and gold.

After a long drought on the prairies, grasshoppers may form swarms, damaging many plants in just a few minutes.

WHERE IN THE WORLD?

Grasslands are found on many of the world's continents. This map shows where the world's major temperate and tropical grasslands are located. Find the place where you live on the map. Which grassland area is nearest you? How do you think grasslands affect the people and economy of the communities near them?

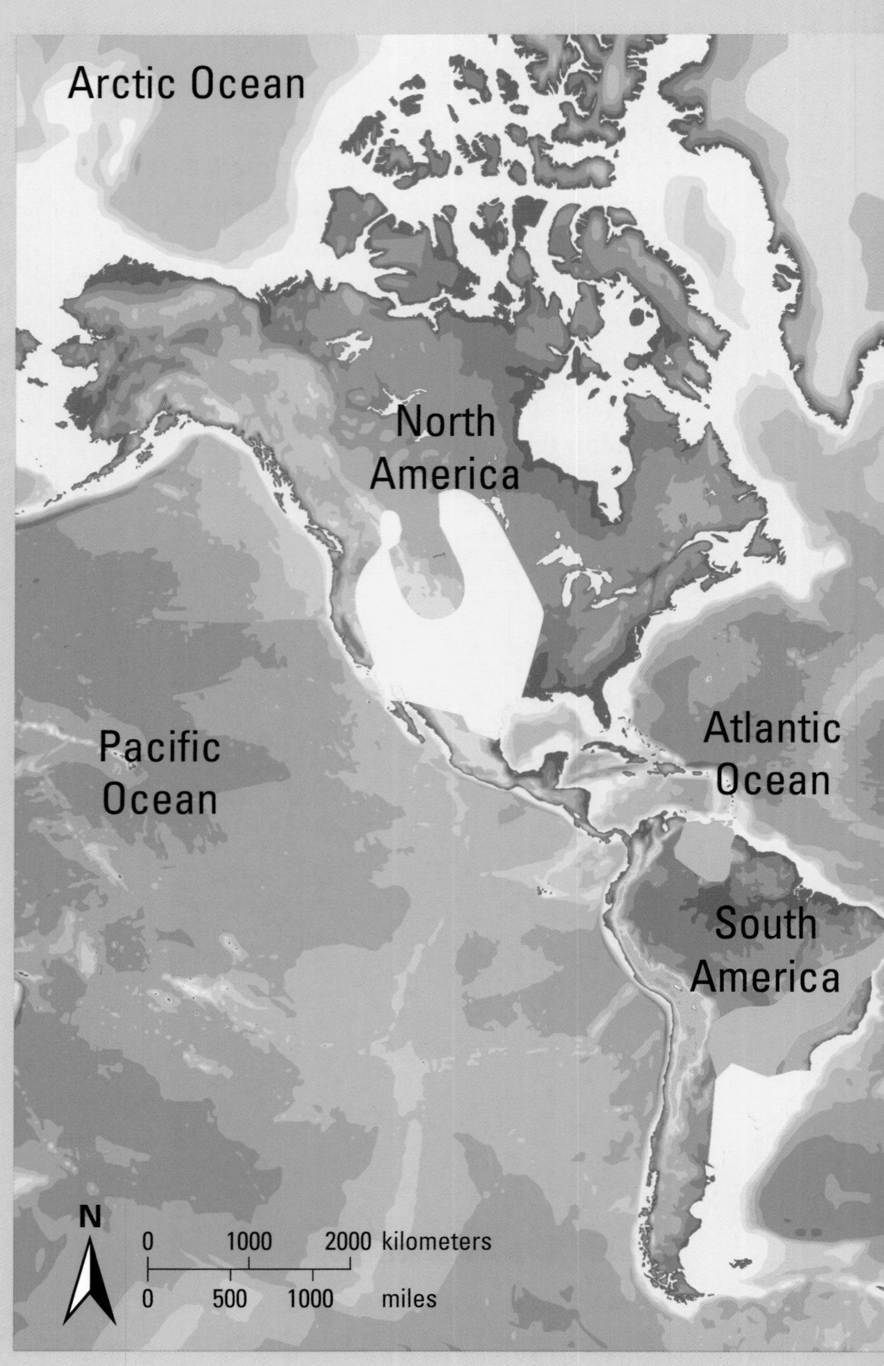

Temperate Grasslands

Savanna/Tropical Grasslands

Arctic Ocean
Asia
Europe
Africa
Pacific Ocean
Atlantic
Ocean
Indian
Ocean
Australia
Southern Ocean

Temperate and Tropical Climates

Grasslands can exist in temperate and tropical climates. The temperate climate of prairie grasslands and Eurasian steppes changes from freezing cold to very hot, depending on the season. Snow often covers the ground, and temperatures can drop below 32° Fahrenheit (0° Celsius). During mid-winter, the temperature may fall below –40° F (–40° C). During mid-summer, temperatures average about 86° F (30° C) and can reach higher than 100° F (38° C). During the late spring and early summer months, the annual average rainfall is about 20 to 35 inches (51 to 89 cm). The steppes, however, receive only 10 to 20 inches (25 to 51 cm) of rainfall.

Savanna grasslands have a tropical climate. Tropical climates are characterized by a wet and a dry season. During the wet season, moist winds blow in from the ocean. Soon, thunderclouds gather, and lightning strikes the ground. Once the rain begins to fall, muddy rivers flow through the savanna, and the land becomes lush with vegetation. Rainfall during the wet season averages 30 to 40 inches (76 to 101 cm). Some areas, such as India, receive very heavy rainfall and strong winds. This is called a **monsoon.** During seasons with little rainfall, the land suffers from drought.

In savanna grasslands, the rainy period is followed by a long, dry course of drought, which is when fires occur. Tropical forests would develop if this cycle was not present.

Grassland fires move quickly and do not stay in one place for very long.

In October, the dry season begins. Strong, dry winds blow across the savanna, removing the moisture of the wet season. During the dry season, the temperature is scorching hot, ranging from 68° F to 86° F (20° to 30° C). In January, extremely dry grass often catches fire. If the ground is very dry, the fire spreads quickly across the land, burning vegetation in its path.

Lightning and careless humans cause many grassland fires. **Poachers** often start fires to clear the land so they can see animals more clearly.

Fires in temperate and tropical grasslands affect **biodiversity**. Fires can prevent some plant species from living and thriving in an area. Shrubs or trees may not be able to grow because fires kill their seedlings. However, fires also help some plant species grow deep roots. This helps the plants retain **nutrients** so that they can sprout when the soil becomes moist.

FASCINATING FACTS

After a fire in the savanna, some grasses grow rapidly—as much as 1 inch (2.5 cm) in 24 hours.

Some trees in the savanna have fire-resistant bark.

Types of Grasslands

Grasslands are sometimes named for the conditions under which they form. The terms *edaphic, climatic,* and *derived* indicate these specific conditions.

Edaphic Grasslands

Special soil conditions in edaphic grasslands restrict the growth of trees. These grasslands are often located on hills or ridges where the soil is shallow. They can also occur in valleys where clay soil becomes waterlogged in the wet season. Soil poor in nutrients can also contribute to the development of edaphic grasslands. Edaphic grasslands do not need fire to maintain the ecosystem.

Grasslands in mountain areas sometimes develop as a result of edaphic conditions such as excessive or limited soil moisture.

It can take 50 years for trees to grow back in an area that has been clear cut.

Climatic Grasslands

Climatic grasslands only form under special climate conditions. Climatic grasslands are usually found in tropical climates. These grasslands require an annual rainfall of about 20 to 50 inches (51 to 125 cm) per year and periods of drought when fires can occur.

Derived Grasslands

Derived grasslands develop in areas that have been **cultivated** by farmers or **clear cut** by forestry companies. To cultivate the land, some farmers clear trees from the area. They plant crops on this land until there is no more fertile soil. Then, they wait 1 year for grasses to cover the land. They burn the grass and plant crops in the ashes. The ashes have many nutrients to feed the crops.

FASCINATING FACTS

Droughts are important to maintaining climatic grasslands. If rain were to be steady throughout the year, the areas would change from grasslands into tropical forests.

Elephants can also create grasslands. Elephants in preserves in Africa have destroyed forested areas by eating leaves and twigs, breaking branches, and smashing the trunks of trees. The tree remains are then removed by fire, and grassland replaces the forested area.

Science in the Grasslands

Scientists work in grasslands research laboratories to discover ways to improve soil fertility and water quality. They use technology to predict crop production and to control weeds. Local farmers also use tools to improve land quality.

Scientific researchers are trying to discover why **herbaceous** plants are changing into woody plants all over the world. Scientists believe an increase in carbon dioxide **emissions** from the atmosphere are causing these plant species and the landscape to change. The plants change to adapt to the higher carbon dioxide levels.

Many associations help farmers and scientists learn how to protect grassland regions. These associations gather important scientific information about agricultural methods. They present awards to farmers and businesses that use the best technology and farming methods. These awards encourage farmers to build better grassland environments for humans, plants, and animals.

Laboratories can perform tests to determine the amount of pollutants or nutrients in soil.

Scientists place plants in different moisture and climate environments to analyze certain conditions.

Recycling rainwater is a good way to preserve grassland regions. In savannas, people build terraces on farmland to catch rainfall. The collected rainwater is used to water crops. Replanting trees is another way to renew the savanna landscape. Rainwater and winds cause soil erosion. Trees help prevent deep ditches or gullies from forming on the land.

FASCINATING FACTS

On the African savanna, agricultural organizations develop techniques to help farmers grow better crops. Some organizations provide farmers with improved seed varieties and information about fertilizers, early planting benefits, and pest control.

In South America, grasses are planted in areas where grass does not naturally grow. The new grasses help lower carbon dioxide levels in the atmosphere. In Brazil, there are more than 86 million acres (35 million hectares) of new grasses.

GRASSLAND PLANTS AND ANIMALS

An ecosystem is a balance of living and non-living things working together to form a community. Invertebrates, such as insects, are part of an ecosystem. Water, soil, and sunshine are also part of the balance of life. Decomposers, such as earthworms, move through the soil, eating dead animal or plant matter. Waste produced by earthworms contains many nutrients for the soil. Plants need these nutrients to survive.

The flowers of butterfly milkweed contain nectar that attracts many butterflies.

PLANTS

In many parts of the world, grasslands are located between forests and deserts. Most grasslands have fewer than one tree per acre (0.40 hectare) of land. Shrubs, grasses, and flowers dominate these biomes. These plants include pampas grass, sweet vernal, and milkweed.

MAMMALS

Grasslands are home to many mammal species. In Africa, elephants, antelopes, and hyenas roam the grasslands. Dingoes, donkeys, and kangaroos live on Australian grasslands. The North-American grasslands are home to wolves, rabbits, bison, and elk. In South America, jaguars, llamas, and opossums live on grasslands. Leopards and voles live on Eurasia's grasslands.

The bison is the largest land animal in North America.

REPTILES AND INVERTEBRATES

Reptiles living in the North-American grasslands include the great plains skink, plains garter snake, and northern prairie skink. The Australian grasslands are home to the pygmy blue-tongued lizard and the eastern brown snake. Many invertebrates live in the grasslands as well. These include the praying mantis, American bird grasshopper, and goldenrod spider. The mourning cloak and eastern black swallowtail are just two of the butterfly species that live on the grasslands.

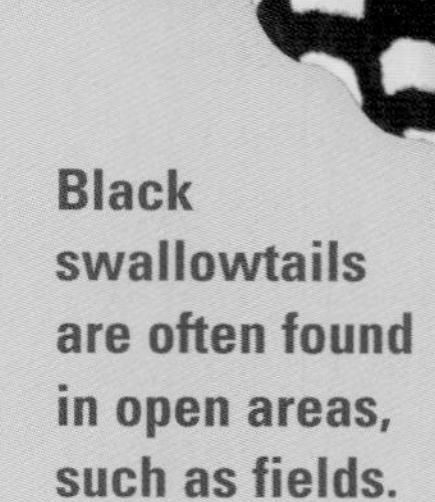

Black swallowtails are often found in open areas, such as fields.

BIRDS

The North-American prairies are home to many bird species that fly among its grasses. Grasshopper sparrows, lark buntings, prairie chickens, and upland sandpipers are just a few of the many birds that live in this area. Birds found in the African savanna include the ostrich and the fork-tailed drongo.

Ostriches can reach a running speed of 45 miles (70 km) per hour.

Temperate and Tropical Grassland Plants

North-American Prairies

Many different grasses grow on the North-American prairies. Buffalo grass grows abundantly throughout the prairies and can survive drought and cold weather. This grass becomes a lavender color in autumn and brown in the winter. Buffalo grass grows in patches 6 to 12 feet (1.8 to 3.7 m) wide. It can be 2 to 5 inches (5 to 13 cm) tall. The North-American prairie is home to many colorful flower species, including the pasque, prairie lily, and wild rose. In autumn, yellow daisies cover the prairie landscape. Milkweed is a flowering plant that grows on the prairies in the summertime. Milkweed grows from 2 to 6 feet (61 to 183 cm) tall. The milkweed's pods contain fluffy seeds that the wind carries to meadows or fields.

The pasque flower blossoms in late March.

Pampas grass blooms when days get shorter.

Eurasian Steppes

The steppes are home to many types of grasses. Depending on the location, the height of the grass varies. If the grasses grow near a forest, they may receive more moisture. Forest grasses can grow up to 4 feet (1.2 m) high. If the grasses are near a desert, they will grow about 1 foot (30 cm) tall. Some plants in the steppe include tumbleweed, rhubarb, and sagebrush.

South-American Pampas

There are a wide variety of plants in the South-American pampas. Pampas grass thrives in the Sun but grows best in damp ground. This grass can grow from 8 to 12 feet (2.4 to 3.7 m) high. Pampas grass is an ornamental grass that is often used for hedges.

Australian Savanna

In the Australian savanna, the jarrah tree, a species of eucalyptus, grows from 131 to 164 feet (40 to 50 m) high. The jarrah tree is hardy and drought resistant. It can live up to 500 years. The wood from the tree is strong and makes sturdy furniture. Jarrah tree flowers have a pleasant scent.

African Savanna

The Senegal gum **acacia** can grow up to 66 feet (20 m) tall. It is a hardy tree that can withstand drought. Gum that is tapped from the tree is used to make a medicinal cream and a type of soda drink. The baobab tree grows near the equator. This tree stores water in its trunk for the dry season. Its bark is fireproof. **Candelabra** trees have branches that point upward, so the tree looks like a candelabra. The candelabra tree's white sap is poisonous. If the sap comes in contact with skin, the skin will blister.

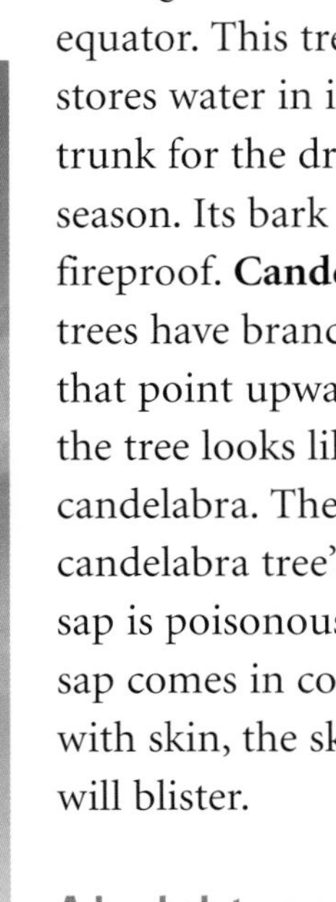

A baobab tree can live for thousands of years.

Pampas grass has sharp leaves. If touched, it may cut skin.

The rose mallee grows in the Australian grasslands. This tree produces a large amount of nectar and has flowers 3 inches (7.5 cm) wide.

Sweet vernal, a rare flowering plant from the Eurasian steppes, is used to make heart medicine.

Temperate Grassland Animals

North-American Prairies

There is an abundance of animal diversity in temperate grasslands. Horses and deer roam the North-American grasslands. The area also includes prairie dogs, coyotes, and bison. Today, most bison live in national parks and on ranches. Only a few bison herds can be found in the wild.

Wild horses feed on the abundance of grasses found on the grasslands.

Australian Grasslands

Kangaroos are large mammals that travel and live in mobs of up to fifty. Kangaroos roam the grasslands searching for food and water. They feed on grass and other small plants. Wallabies and wombats make their homes in the Australian grasslands, too. The emu is a large bird that travels the Australian grasslands searching for insects, seeds, lizards, or rodents to eat. This bird has long legs and stands 6 feet (1.8 m) tall.

Eurasian Steppes

The Eurasian steppes are home to small, grass-eating rodents, such as hamsters, gerbils, and mice. Predators include coyotes, badgers, and foxes. Corsac foxes live in the steppes of Central Asia. They live in burrows and eat birds, plants, reptiles, and other small animals.

Wombats have been exterminated in some places because they are believed to ruin crops.

South-American Pampas

Viscachas live in the pampas of South America. Viscachas are burrowing rodents that grow as large as guinea pigs. Geoffrey's cats also live in the pampas of Argentina in South America. With their stripes and spots, Geoffrey's cats look like pet cats. Geoffrey's cats appear to walk upside-down when climbing a tree branch. They hang onto branches using their back feet.

FASCINATING FACTS

Some hunters kill Geoffrey's cats for their fur. It takes twenty-five Geoffrey's cats' skins to make one fur coat.

Prairie dogs are sociable animals that build connecting burrows. When they see each other, they kiss.

The bison was nearly extinct at the beginning of the 1900s due to overhunting. Today, there are about 20,000 bison on the plains.

Kangaroos can hop up to 19 miles (30 km) per hour. When an enemy approaches a group of kangaroos, each animal hops in a different direction.

Viscachas live in groups of up to thirty individuals.

Tropical Grassland Animals

African Savanna

Many animals live on the tropical grasslands of Africa. Weighing up to 10,000 pounds (4,536 kg), African, or savanna, elephants are large creatures with ivory tusks and long trunks. They use their strong teeth to feed on shrubs, bark, grasses, and fruit. The lion is a powerful creature that weighs 265 to 420 pounds (120 to 191 kg). Lions roam the African savanna searching for buffalo, zebra, or gazelle to eat. Running at 40 miles (64 km) per hour, the lion can chase its prey easily. Grant's zebras also live on the African plains. They live in groups of up to seventeen individuals.

Dingoes hunt for birds, rats, and rabbits at night.

The African elephant eats about 496 pounds (225 kg) of vegetation a day.

Australian Savanna

A wild dog called the dingo makes its home in the Australian savanna. Dingoes are ginger-brown in color and weigh about 33 pounds (15 kg). These dogs do not bark. They communicate by howling and coughing. Koalas can also be found in savanna areas. Koalas have brown fur that blends in with their environment. This helps them avoid predators, such as dingoes. A diverse number of reptiles, such as the saltwater crocodile, live on this savanna, too.

South-American Savanna

Greater rheas are birds that live in the eastern part of South America. These birds cannot fly, but they run quickly. Standing 5 feet (1.5 m) tall, greater rheas weigh about 50 pounds (23 kg). The capybara is also found in the savanna of South America. The capybara is the largest living rodent, with a body length ranging from 42 to 53 inches (107 to 135 cm), a height of 20 to 24 inches (51 to 61 cm), and a weight of between 77 and 140 (35 and 64 kg) pounds.

The greater rhea is almost full grown at 5 months.

FASCINATING FACTS

A group of lions is called a pride. Most often, female lions are the hunters for the pride.

The African elephant is the world's largest land mammal.

Zebras weigh between 385 and 850 pounds (129 to 386 kg).

Baby koalas, or joeys, are only 0.8 inches (2 cm) long when they are born.

Endangered Grassland Plants and Animals

Plants and animals in danger of becoming extinct are classified as endangered. This means there are so few of the species alive that they need protection to survive. Kangaroo grass, wallaby grass, the pygmy blue-tongued lizard, and the Mexican prairie dog are just a few of the grasslands plants and animals that are endangered. In the United States, people are not allowed to hunt or harm endangered animals.

In some places, human development is destroying the environment. Conservation councils help raise awareness about such destruction and take steps to save the environment. In central Wisconsin, a project called the Central Wisconsin Grassland Conservation Area aims to protect 15,000 acres (6,000 ha) of grassland. The project is also trying to save the greater prairie chicken from becoming extinct.

Like many lizards, the pygmy blue-tongued lizard can smell through its nostrils and tongue.

The Craigieburn Grassland Conservation Reserve near Melbourne, Australia, has 840 acres (340 ha) of native grassland. At the Gilbertsons Grassland Reserve, there are five threatened plant species as well as the striped legless lizard, which is in danger of becoming extinct. Another Australian grasslands reserve, Bannockburn Cemetery, has many endangered plants, including the yam daisy, button wrinklewort, and large-fruit groundsel.

The African savanna has many conservation reserves, too. In South Africa, the Kruger and Kalahari Gemsbok National Parks are reserve lands geared toward protecting the area's native plants and animals. In these places, conservation groups are re-seeding native plants and protecting animals.

Safari tours provide people with the opportunity to learn about wildlife and nature.

GRASSLAND STUDIES

Working in the grasslands is challenging. From farming to conservation and restoration projects, the work is difficult because of the extreme environments within the biome. Before delving into a grassland career, knowledge of conservation issues, grassland ecology, and vegetation is strongly recommended. Research careers in the grasslands by visiting the public library or surfing the Internet.

GRASSLANDS MANAGER

- Duties: develops conservation methods to promote ecosystem health
- Education: bachelor of science degree in wildlife management, master of science degree in animal ecology, fire boss certification
- Interests: natural communities, plants, animals, and restoration ecology

The grasslands manager's job requires managerial skills to hire and work with volunteers, firefighting crews, and short-term seasonal workers. The grasslands manager also works with other conservation organizations to make plans to improve the ecosystem.

FIELD RESEARCH BIOLOGIST

- Duties: studies animal habits and habitats
- Education: bachelor of science in wildlife management, master of science in natural resource management
- Interests: wildlife, habitats

Field research biologists explore and monitor animals in their environment. Field researchers sometimes trap birds and release them in places that have fewer birds. This allows the population to grow.

CONSULTANT ENVIRONMENTAL SCIENTIST

- Duties: assesses causes of habitat loss in many biomes, including grasslands
- Education: degree in environmental biology, environmental engineering diploma
- Interests: biomes, conservation, biodiversity

Environmental scientists collect data about water, air, and soil quality. They study the data, then give advice and suggestions about how to clean the environment.

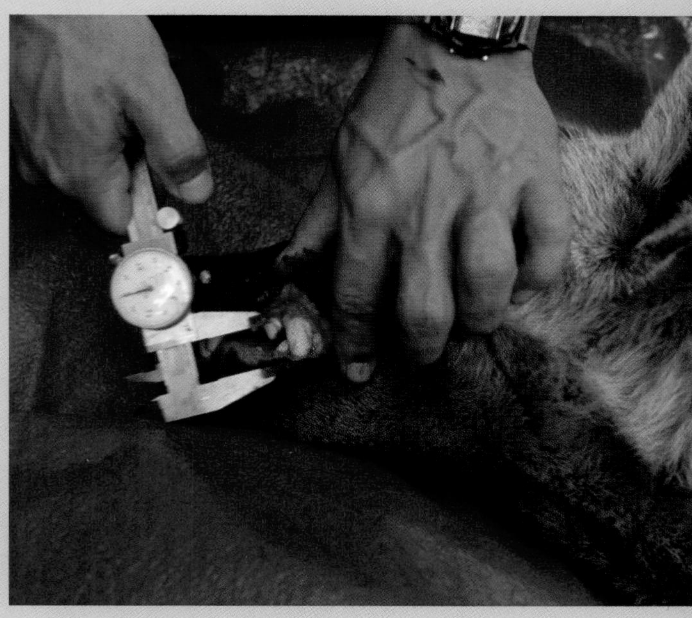

ECO CHALLENGE

1. Name the two main categories of grasslands.
2. What defines tropical grasslands?
3. What are the five major areas of grasslands in the world?
4. Name the seasons of the temperate grasslands and the tropical grasslands.
5. What are the main causes of fire in the grasslands?

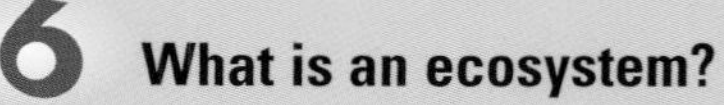

6 **What is an ecosystem?**

7 **Name two invertebrates that live on the grasslands.**

8 **How do dingoes communicate?**

9 **Which African animal helps make grasslands?**

10 **Name two endangered grasslands animals.**

Answers

1. temperate and tropical
2. climate
3. the prairies of North America, the steppes of central Eurasia, the veldt of South Africa, the deserts in Australia, and the pampas of South America
4. The temperate grassland seasons are summer, winter, spring, and fall. The tropical grassland seasons are the wet and the dry seasons.
5. lightning and human carelessness
6. An ecosystem is a community of non-living and living organisms interacting with each other.
7. earthworms and butterflies
8. by howling and coughing
9. elephant
10. pygmy blue-tongued lizard, Mexican prairie dog

CREATE A GRASSLAND

To stimulate a patch of grassland, try growing wheat grass in your own home or classroom.

MATERIALS

- Paper towel
- Water
- Wheat grass seeds
- Bowl
- Potting soil
- 2 seed trays
- Plastic grassland animals

1. Moisten paper towel with water. Place wheat grass seeds in the paper towel.
2. Place the moistened paper towel and the seeds in the bowl. Let them sit for 6 to 12 hours or until they sprout.
3. Place potting soil in seed trays. Put the sprouted wheat grass seeds in the trays. Cover with more soil. Moisten with water.
4. When the wheat grass reaches about 6 inches (15 cm), put plastic grassland animals in the grass on both trays to create a savanna and prairie.
5. Place the trays on display. Discuss which animals belong on the savanna and which ones belong on the prairies.

Mold may grow between the blades of grass. Do not eat the wheat grass.

FURTHER RESEARCH

How can I find more information about ecosystems, grasslands, animals, and plants?

- Libraries have many interesting books about ecosystems, grasslands, animals, and plants.
- Science centers and research facilities are great places to learn about ecosystems, grasslands, animals, and plants.
- The Internet offers some great Web sites dedicated to ecosystems, grasslands, animals, and plants.

BOOKS

Bethar, Susie. *Grasslands.* Brookfield, CT: Copper Beech, 2000.

Collard, Sneed B. *The Prairie Builders: Reconstructing America's Lost Grasslands.* Boston, MA: Houghton Mifflin, 2005.

Wallace, Marianne D. *America's Prairies and Grasslands: Guide to Plants and Animals.* Golden, CO: Fulcrum Publishing, 2001.

WEB SITES

Where can I learn more about grassland biomes of the world?

Grassland Biomes
www.worldbiomes.com/biomes_grassland.htm

Where can I learn more about prairies?

Prairies Forever
www.prairies.org

Where can I learn about the many animals of the grasslands?

Grassland Animals
http://mbgnet.mobot.org/sets/grasslnd/animals

GLOSSARY

acacia: a spiny, fire-resistant tree

biodiversity: the number of species of plants or animals found in a biome

candelabra: an ornamental candle holder that holds more than one candle

clear cut: to cut down all the trees in a section of forest

cultivated: prepared land for planting by fertilizing or plowing

decomposers: organisms, such as bacteria, that digest the remains of dead plants and animals

drought: a time when there is little or no rain and the land dries up

ecosystem: a community of living things sharing an environment

emissions: gases or other pollutants that are discharged into the air

herbaceous: non-woody plant

invertebrates: animals that do not have a backbone

monsoon: a period of heavy rainfall that is carried by wind to southern Asia

nutrients: substances that provide nourishment

organisms: individual life forms

poachers: people who illegally hunt animals

INDEX